THINKING *Higher* THAN TROPHIES

SINAI JAGDALE

THINKING HIGHER THAN TROPHIES

CONTENTS

Introduction

"Thinking Higher than the Trophies"

INTRODUCTION

We are all performers in the vast theatre of life, each playing our unique roles, striving for success, and navigating the complex dynamics of competition and collaboration. From the playground to the boardroom, from classrooms to corporate arenas, the interplay between competition and cooperation shapes our interactions, influences our decisions, and defines our journey toward personal and collective growth.

In this book, we embark on a journey to explore the intricate dance between competition and collaboration, unravelling their variations, understanding their impacts, and discovering the profound lessons they offer through insightful reflections, real-life anecdotes, and practical knowledge, we delve into the heart of human interaction, shedding light on how these forces shape our relationships, drive innovation and fuel our aspirations.

Thinking Higher than Trophies

From the emotion-fueled rush of competition to the harmonious symphony of collaboration, we examine the various facets of human endeavor, celebrating triumphs, confronting challenges, and embracing the transformative power of working together towards common goals. Drawing from psychology, sociology, and personal experiences, we uncover the hidden truths behind our quest for success, unravelling the mysteries of the human psyche and lighting up the path toward fulfilment and achievement.

As we navigate through the following chapters, let us embark on a voyage of self-discovery, embracing the lessons of competition and collaboration as guiding stars in our journey toward personal excellence and collective prosperity. Together, let us unravel the secrets of success, forge meaningful connections, and chart a course toward a brighter tomorrow, where collaboration triumphs over competition and unity paves the way for boundless possibilities.

Join me as we embark on this odyssey of exploration and enlightenment, where every page reveals new insights, every chapter unlocks new perspectives, and every word inspires us to strive for greatness, not only for ourselves but for the world we inhabit.

Welcome to the adventure of a lifetime...

Chapter 1

"Beyond Victory: The True Meaning of Competition"

"Thinking Higher than the Trophies"

CHAPTER 1

BEYOND VICTORY- The True Meaning of Competition

Competition is the act of striving to outperform others to achieve a desired outcome. Since the foundation of humanity, competition has been an undeniable part of the human race. It fosters innovation and drives individuals to surpass their limitations, leading to advancements in various fields such as technology, sports, and business. Competition has always helped humans rethink their abilities and skills, motivating them to strive for improvement.

Additionally, competition fuels a sense of motivation and determination among individuals, spurring them to work harder on a particular problem. For example, in the field of technology, competition among companies like Apple and Samsung have led to the development of new and improved smartphones with advanced features. In sports, competition pushes athletes to break world records and achieve once-impossible feats.

Two builders, for instance, are mindful of one another's competitiveness. When one of the builders builds a high-quality building, the other builder becomes fearful of competition and builds even better facilities in the building. One meaning I came across when looking up the definition of "competition" on Google or in a dictionary was "rivalry." Furthermore, as we delve further to understand the meaning of "rivalry," one of the definitions we uncover is "fighting."

This suggests that the builders' competitiveness stems from a desire to outdo each other and establish dominance in their field. This constant drive to surpass one another leads to the construction of superior buildings and creates a tense atmosphere of rivalry and potential conflict between the two builders. So, if we connect the dots, we can find the steps of "competition." Competition is a fundamental aspect of human nature and society.

It is the driving force behind innovation, progress, and growth. Whether in sports, business, or academics, competition pushes individuals and organizations to strive for excellence and achieve their full potential.

Steps of Competition:

(How Competition Occupies Our Mind)

First Step of Competition: Being afraid of people better than you.

Second Step of Competition: Trying to make yourself better.

Third Step of Competition: Trying to compete with others.

Fourth Step of Competition:

Competition Turning into Rivalry (Fighting)

By connecting these steps, we can understand the dynamics of competition and its impact on our lives. Let's Understand the Steps of Competition because this progression takes us through the stages of the competition, like a narrative of human endeavour.

First Step:

The first stage begins with an acknowledgement of those who excel, an acknowledgement that sometimes instils a sense of nervousness. This initial step involves being mindful of individuals who are better, faster, or more proficient. This awareness can serve as motivation to improve one's skills and abilities. It is essential to embrace this step with humility and a willingness to learn from those who have already achieved success. It's a recognition that someone out there may surpass us in our chosen domain.

Second Step:

The second stage of competition finds us looking inward, introspecting, and pondering how to improve ourselves. It's a journey of self-discovery, pushing us to break through the barriers of dissatisfaction and mediocrity. This is where we start to sharpen our skills and distil our abilities in our exploration for self-advancement. In this stage, we embrace the idea that growth and progress are continuous processes. We understand that there is always room for improvement and strive to cultivate a growth mindset. As we push ourselves to new limits, we become more resilient and adaptable, ready to face any challenges that come our way. Here is where we begin honing our craft and refining our abilities in the search for personal growth. We can expand our knowledge and expertise by seeking out new challenges and opportunities. This stage is crucial for developing a solid foundation and building upon our existing skills, ultimately propelling us towards achieving our goals and reaching our full potential. As we delve deeper into this stage, we discover our weaknesses and embrace the opportunity to turn them into strengths. It is a time of self-reflection and critical analysis, where we strive to identify areas for improvement and set goals for our personal development. With each step forward, we gain a clearer understanding of our true potential and the path toward reaching it. But do you know? Most people at this stage exclude the search for their weaknesses. And try to compete without being fully prepared. They may fear acknowledging their shortcomings, which can be uncomfortable and challenging. However, by embracing this stage and actively seeking out areas for improvement, we can become more well-rounded individuals who are better equipped to face challenges and achieve success. We must prioritize self-awareness and personal growth to reach our full potential.

Third Step:

In the third stage, the wheels of competition are set in motion as we enter the battlefield with our peers and rivals. We actively contest for recognition, acknowledgement, or the elusive first place. This stage should be handled carefully, as it exemplifies the spirit of competition in its traditional form, where we measure ourselves against others, seeking to surpass their achievements. For example, in a business setting, the third stage could be seen in a group of start-ups competing for funding from venture capitalists. Each start-up is fighting for recognition and acknowledgement as the most promising investment opportunity, striving to surpass its competitors in terms of revenue projections, market share, and customer gain. And if we don't handle this stage carefully, it can lead to unhealthy competition and a toxic work environment. Excessive focus on surpassing others can hinder teamwork and hinder overall growth. This brings us to the fourth stage of the competition. To avoid going to the fourth stage, we should remember that it is crucial to remember that success should not solely be measured by surpassing others but also by personal growth and fulfilment. But, still, we will see the fourth stage, as it will guide you through the consequences of not handling the third stage properly.

Fourth Step:

Competition up to the third stage is fine. But in the fourth stage, the final step is where things can get even more dangerous. Competition can get more intense and become a higher-stakes game where conflicts arise when rivalry grows. Rivalry is the height of competition—the point at which a fierce desire to succeed takes over. Sometimes, it manifests as a physical or mental struggle motivated by a burning desire for achievement. People may go to tremendous lengths at this stage to surpass their rivals, which increases pressure and stress. This heightened pressure and stress can lead to declining sportsmanship and ethical behaviour as individuals focus solely on winning at any cost. This stage can also bring your "office stress' at home. And it may also bring out tension in your family. A tense environment may result from each participant's intense drive for success, which makes them willing to do whatever it takes to succeed. For example, in a corporate setting, two employees competing for a promotion may engage in aggressive behaviour and sabotage each other's work to gain an advantage. This can create a a toxic work environment that is detrimental to overall team productivity and morale. This can create a stressful work environment and negatively impact team dynamics.

(Summary of the Above Concept)

The four steps of competition are acknowledging superiors, trying to improve oneself, attempting to compete with others, and turning competition into rivalry (fighting). This intense drive for success can create a tense environment, leading to aggressive behaviour and negative team dynamics. By connecting these steps, we can understand the dynamics of competition and its impact on our lives.

Origin of the competitive spirit:

The origin of the competitive spirit can be traced back to various aspects of human history. Competition can be seen as deeply rooted in human evolution, stemming from the struggle for survival and the need to secure resources for sustenance. This primal instinct has contributed to the development of a competitive nature in humans. Throughout history, competition has been a driving force behind innovation and progress. It has fuelled advancements in technology, sports, and even academic pursuits. The desire to outperform others and achieve success has shaped societies and individuals. One example that showcases the deep-rooted nature of competition in human evolution is the development of agriculture. In ancient times, as hunter-gatherer societies transitioned to settled farming communities, competition among groups became crucial for securing fertile land and resources. This drive to outdo one another led to innovations in farming techniques, irrigation systems, and crop selection, resulting in more efficient food production and societal progress.

How has competition impacted our society?

One example of the impact of competition on society is the development of capitalism. Capitalism, with its emphasis on market competition, has led to economic growth and wealth creation. This competition between businesses drives innovation and efficiency, ultimately benefiting consumers through lower prices and improved products and services. This has also led to income inequality and the exploitation of workers in some cases. Overall, competition has played a critical role in shaping our society, both positively and negatively. On one hand, it has spurred advancements in technology, medicine, and other industries, leading to a higher standard of living for many. On the other hand, competition has also fueled greed, corruption, and unethical practices in some sectors, causing harm to both individuals and the environment. In essence, while competition can be a powerful force for progress, it must be balanced with regulations and ethical considerations to ensure that it benefits society as a whole.

How competition affects our psychology:

Competition can significantly impact our psychology in various ways, both positively and negatively. Positively, competition can drive individuals to push themselves to achieve their goals, leading to personal growth and success. It can also foster a sense of motivation and drive to excel in a competitive environment. However, competition can also have negative effects on mental health, causing stress, anxiety, and feelings of inadequacy in individuals who feel they are falling behind. Individuals need to find a healthy balance between competition and self-care to ensure their mental well-being is not compromised. Here are some ways competition can affect our psychology:

Motivation and Drive:

Competition can fuel motivation and drive, pushing individuals to work harder and strive for excellence. The desire to win or succeed can be a powerful motivational force that propels individuals to set and achieve challenging goals. For example, in a sports competition, athletes may push themselves to train harder and improve their skills to outperform their opponents and achieve success. This drive for excellence can increase self-confidence and a sense of accomplishment. On the other hand, competition can also have adverse effects on psychology. It can create feelings of stress, anxiety, and self-doubt, especially when individuals compare themselves to others.

Stress and Anxiety:

On the flip side, competition can also lead to heightened levels of stress and anxiety. The pressure to perform well or outdo others can create a sense of constant pressure, leading to increased stress levels that can be detrimental to mental and physical well-being. A decline in mental well-being. For example, in a competitive academic environment, students may constantly compare their grades and achievements to those of their peers, creating an unhealthy sense of competition and pressure to excel continuously. This can result in increased stress levels, a fear of failure, and even the development of mental health issues such as depression or anxiety.

Self-Esteem and Confidence:

Success in a competitive environment can boost self-esteem and confidence, especially when individuals achieve their desired goals or emerge victorious. This increased self-esteem and confidence can lead to a positive mindset and a willingness to take on new challenges. It can also improve overall mental well-being and contribute to a sense of personal fulfilment. For example, a person with high self-esteem and confidence may be more likely to pursue their goals and take risks. They may have the belief in themselves to overcome obstacles and setbacks, leading them to achieve success in their personal and professional lives. However, failure or consistently losing in a competitive setting can significantly impact self-esteem, leading to feelings of inadequacy and self-doubt. These negative emotions can hinder personal growth and discourage individuals from taking risks or pursuing their goals. It is important to create a supportive and encouraging environment that celebrates both successes and failures as learning opportunities. By fostering a culture of resilience and perseverance, individuals can develop a stronger sense of self-worth and belief in their abilities, ultimately leading to greater personal satisfaction and fulfilment. This can be seen in the example of a student who was once shy and lacked confidence.

After participating in a public speaking competition and winning first place, they experienced a boost in their self-esteem. This newfound confidence empowered them to join various clubs and organizations, take on leadership roles, and excel academically. They went on to achieve their dream of attending a prestigious university and pursuing a successful career, all because of a positive mindset.

Social Comparison:

Engaging in competitive activities often involves comparing oneself with others. This constant social comparison can influence one's self-perception and identity, leading to either an inflated or diminished sense of self-worth based on how one measures up against others. This process of social comparison can also impact one's behaviour and motivation. Individuals may strive to outperform others to enhance their self-esteem. One example of social comparison is when individuals compare their physical appearance to that of others on social media platforms. For instance, seeing a friend's perfectly edited and filtered photo may lead someone to feel insecure about their appearance and feel the need to strive for unrealistic beauty standards.

Aggression and enmity:

Intense competition can sometimes lead to heightened aggression and hostility. Mainly, when individuals become overly invested in winning or outperforming others, this can result in strained interpersonal relationships and even conflict (as discussed earlier). This aggression and hostility can manifest in various ways, such as verbal arguments, physical altercations, or even interference in others' efforts. It is important to promote a healthy competitive environment that emphasizes collaboration and respect and prevent the negative consequences of excessive aggression and hostility.
For example, in a workplace setting, if employees are solely focused on outperforming their colleagues to receive recognition or promotions, it can create a toxic work environment. This may lead to employees undermining each other's work, engaging in office politics, and ultimately hindering the overall productivity of the team. However, by fostering a

competitive but collaborative culture where individuals support and encourage each other's growth, teams can achieve higher levels of success while maintaining positive relationships. Overall, the impact of competition on an individual's psychology depends on various factors, including the nature of the competition, individual personality traits, and the broader social and cultural context in which the competition takes place. It is essential to strike a balance between healthy competition and the well-being of individuals to ensure a positive psychological impact.

(Summary of the 1st Chapter)

Competition is the act of striving to outperform others to achieve a desired outcome, and it has been an undeniable part of human nature since the foundation of humanity. It fosters innovation, drives individuals to surpass their limitations, and leads to advancements in various fields such as technology, sports, and business. Competition fuels a sense of motivation and determination among individuals, spurring them to work harder on a particular problem. The steps to competition are:

1. Acknowledging those who excel:

This initial step involves being mindful of those who are better, faster, or more proficient. This awareness can serve as motivation to improve one's skills and abilities.

2. Introspection:

This second stage of competition finds us looking inward, introspecting, and pondering how to improve ourselves. This journey of self-discovery pushes us to break through barriers of dissatisfaction and mediocrity.

3. Trying to make ourselves better:

This third stage of competition sets the wheels of competition in motion as we enter the battlefield with our peers and rivals. This stage should be handled carefully, as it exemplifies the spirit of competition in its most traditional form, where we measure ourselves against others, seeking to surpass their achievements.

4. Rivalry (fighting):

This fourth and final step is where things can get even more dangerous. Competition can get more intense and turn into a higher-stakes game where conflicts can arise when rivalry grows. This stage can lead to heightened pressure and stress, which can lead to a decline in sportsmanship and ethical behaviour.

Conclusion:

In the grand tapestry of human existence, competition stands as both a testament to our aspirations and a crucible of our tribulations. From its humble origins amidst the primordial struggle for survival to its modern manifestations in the realms of technology, sports, and commerce, competition remains an indelible force shaping the course of humanity.

Chapter 2

"Under the Sun"

"Thinking Higher than the Trophies"

CHAPTER 2

"UNDER THE SUN"

"**Under the Sun.**" You might be wondering: What does this phrase mean? This phrase is often used in very diverse contexts. But, in this book, you will see a new and reinvigorated idea about this phrase: under the sun. "Under the Sun" in this book refers to our "Thinking" or "Thought" process. We typically limit our thinking to certain boundaries. Why do we confine our thinking to such narrow perspectives? "Under the Sun" challenges us to explore the endless possibilities and potential that lie beyond these self-

imposed boundaries. Many people think competition is just rivalry or a fight for superiority. But why stay so limited? Instead, we should expand our understanding of competition. By doing so, we can uncover new insights and opportunities for growth and collaboration. Why not explore the idea that competition can also be a catalyst for personal growth and self-improvement?

By broadening our perspective "under the sun," we open ourselves up to new possibilities and opportunities for collaboration and innovation.

(A New View of Competition)

We can view competition as a forging tool that consistently edifies us to adapt to certain situations. For example, plants and animals also compete with each other for nourishment and shelter. But do they fight with each other? No, instead, they adapt themselves to the nature of that competitor. They evolve and develop new strategies to thrive in their environment. Similarly, by embracing competition as a catalyst for growth, we can learn from our competitors and adapt our approaches to become more resilient and successful. Rather than engaging in confrontation or hostility, we can learn from nature and adapt our skills and strategies to stay ahead. By observing how plants and animals coexist and thrive, we can understand the importance of collaboration, innovation, and continuous improvement in the face of competition. This approach not only benefits us individually but also fosters a healthier and more productive work environment overall. Doesn't this teach us a significant thing? Yes, it does. What's that significant thing? The significant thing is that, in our workplace, yes, we have a competitor. Whoever always tries to compete with us and tries to assert that he or she is superior to or better than us We also take part in that race and try to show, "How are we better than them?" But, in this race, even though we are more promising than them, some fail and some succeed. In this case, we should take a step back and evaluate our competitors. And be like plants and animals who adapt themselves to the nature of their competitors. Yes, we should not "adapt to the competitor" but instead adapt to the "nature of the competitor." What is the difference between "adapting to the competitor" and "adapting to the nature of the competitor"?

Adapting to the Competition:

Adapting to the competition means giving up and not persevering to be a better version of yourself. Later, this will take a turn to depression or thinking about the same thing again and again. In this case, the competitor will be happier to see you in this state. It is important to remember that competition should not solely define your self-worth or happiness. Instead of giving up, focus on embracing your unique strengths and continuously improving yourself. By staying true to your journey and personal growth, you can find fulfilment and contentment, regardless of what the competitor may think or feel.

Adapting to the Nature of Competitor:

Adapting to the nature of the competitor means that some people have that inbuilt nature of backbiting without any reason. So, "adapting to the nature of the competitor" means taking a step back and adapting to the nature of the competitor. This in turn will make the competitor think, "How is this person not affected by my competition?" Because of this practice of "taking a step back," you will always be prepared to fight with others too. Adapting to the nature of the competitor requires developing a strategic mindset that focuses on one's strengths and goals rather than getting caught up in unnecessary conflicts. By maintaining a calm and composed demeanour, one can effectively navigate through competitive environments and stay focused on their success. This approach not only allows for better decision-making but also builds a reputation of professionalism and resilience, ultimately leading to long-term success in any competitive field. Have you ever seen a boxing match? What does the experienced boxer do? He waits for the opponent to be tired and then plays his or her magical move to make the opponent lose badly. Similarly, in competitive environments, individuals with a calm and composed demeanour understand the importance of patience and strategic timing. They observe their surroundings, waiting for the right moment to make their move and capitalize on opportunities. By doing so, they can effectively outmanoeuvre their competition and achieve their goals with precision and finesse. This ability to patiently assess the situation and strike at the opportune moment sets them apart as experienced contenders in any competitive field. The same holds for a lion too. Whenever a lion wants to attack his prey, he takes a step back and then assails his prey. Now, you have to decide: Are you a lion or a prey?

So, as you navigate the competitive arena, envision yourself not just as a participant but as a strategist, a lion strategically biding its time. The lion recognizes that true potency lies not just in the roar but in the art of choosing the right moment to take a step back and pounce. "Under the Sun" will help you think "Above the Sun." "Above the Sun" will make you a farsighted person who will have the pre-conscience of being able to fight tough competition. This approach not only allows for better decision-making but also builds a reputation of professionalism and resilience, ultimately leading to long-term success in any competitive field. By understanding the importance of timing and strategic retreats, individuals can effectively assess their surroundings and make calculated moves that maximize their chances of success. This ability to navigate challenges with a composed and calculated approach sets individuals apart from their competitors and positions them as leaders in their respective fields. Moreover, cultivating a reputation for professionalism and resilience not only opens doors to new opportunities but also fosters trust and respect among peers, creating a solid foundation for long-term success.

(Summary of the 2nd Chapter)

"Under the Sun" is a phrase that challenges us to explore the endless possibilities and potential that lie beyond our self-imposed boundaries. It encourages us to expand our understanding of competition, which can be a catalyst for personal growth and self- improvement. Competition can be viewed as a forging tool that consistently edifies us to adapt to certain situations. By observing how plants and animals coexist and thrive, we can understand the importance of collaboration, innovation, and continuous improvement in the face of competition. In the workplace, we have competitors who constantly try to compete with us, asserting their superiority. Instead of giving up, we should focus on embracing our unique strengths and continuously improving ourselves. Adapting to the nature of the competitor means taking a step back and adapting to the nature of the competitor, making the competitor think, "How is this person not affected by my competition?" This practice of "taking a step back" allows us to navigate through competitive environments and stay focused on our success. By thinking "above the sun," we can become farsighted people who can fight tough competition, leading to better decision-making and a reputation of professionalism and resilience.

Conclusion:

In the grand symphony of life, competition is but one movement—a melody of challenges and triumphs. "Under the Sun" invites us to transcend the cacophony of rivalry and embrace the harmony of collaboration and growth. By reimagining competition as a crucible for adaptation and innovation, we unlock the door to boundless possibilities and collective advancement.

Thinking Higher than Trophies

Quote:

"You should step into the competitive field when you are fully equipped and have the mentality to face your rival with the mind-set of a lion, not a prey."

-Sinai Jagdale (author)

Chapter 3

"Together We Compete:
The Power of Collective Ambition"

"Thinking Higher than the Trophies"

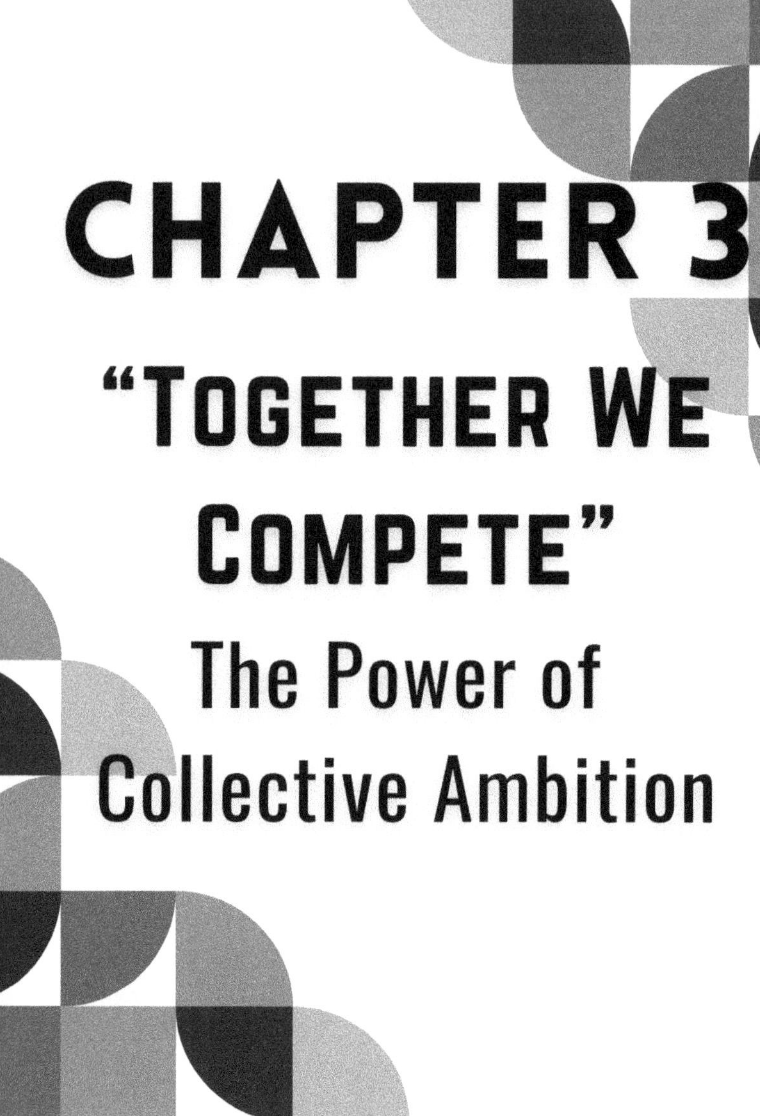

CHAPTER 3

"TOGETHER WE COMPETE"

The Power of Collective Ambition

"**Collaborative competition**" is a term that may seem contradictory at first, as competition and collaboration are often viewed as opposing concepts. However, the idea behind collaborative competition is to blend elements of both collaboration and competition to accomplish common goals or mutual benefits. This approach can foster innovation and creativity by bringing together diverse perspectives and skill sets. By working together towards a shared objective, individuals and organizations can push each other to achieve their best while still maintaining a sense of camaraderie and mutual respect. In this way, collaborative competition can lead to a win-win situation where all parties involved can thrive and grow. In all these chapters, we have seen both sides of a competition, how to overcome the "under the sun" thinking process, etc. But, in this chapter, we will see a fresh idea of how competition can turn productive.

In this chapter, we will explore the concept of productive competition, which involves harnessing the positive aspects of competition to drive innovation and improve performance. Productive competition recognizes that healthy competition can fuel creativity, inspire individuals to push their limits, and spur innovation. By encouraging individuals or teams to compete constructively, organizations can foster a culture of continuous improvement and achieve greater success. This chapter will delve into strategies for promoting productive competition and harnessing its potential to drive positive outcomes. By encouraging individuals or teams to compete constructively, organizations can foster creativity, enhance productivity, and ultimately achieve greater success. This approach recognizes that healthy competition can spur individuals to push their limits, learn from one another, and collectively strive for excellence.

Collaborative Competition This concept has helped many individuals who are working for or running a company. This concept is a way to experience healthy competition. This idea includes a plan in which both individuals have to agree on each other's ideas. We have often heard the proverb, "Two heads are better than one." In the same way, in collaborative competition, the work is done more productively and efficiently because individuals are working on the same project. Collaborative competition fosters a sense of teamwork and encourages individuals to leverage their unique strengths and skills to achieve a common goal. By combining different perspectives and expertise, this approach promotes innovation and problem-solving, ultimately leading to better outcomes. Additionally, this concept promotes a supportive environment where individuals can learn from each other and grow both personally and professionally. For example, in a marketing team, instead of each member working independently on different campaigns, they collaborate and compete against another team to come up with the best overall marketing strategy. Through sharing ideas, pooling resources, and leveraging each other's strengths, the team can create a more comprehensive and impactful campaign that yields better results than if they had worked alone. This concept promotes cooperation and innovation and drives individuals to push their limits while still fostering a supportive and collaborative environment. By encouraging collaboration and healthy competition, this approach also fosters a sense of unity among team members. It allows individuals to learn from one another, develop new skills, and gain a deeper understanding of the various industries as a whole. Ultimately, this dynamic environment leads to continuous improvement and the ability to adapt to ever-changing trends. And because individuals work together, the result is also unique and diverse. Ultimately, this diversity fosters creativity and innovation.

Healthy competition and cooperation are essential elements for stimulating growth, innovation, and progress in various aspects of life. Have you ever been to a chemistry lab? In the chemistry lab, certain chemicals work well with each other. Some chemicals are reactive when they come together. In the same way, we have to observe who can collaborate with us nicely. Otherwise, the collaboration turns into extreme and intense chaos. By understanding our strengths and weaknesses, we can better assess who we work well with and who may not be the best fit. Just like in chemistry lab, where certain combinations create powerful reactions, finding the right collaborators can lead to incredible results. It's important to strike a balance between healthy competition and cooperation to drive progress and innovation forward. So, next time you consider a collaboration, choose your partners wisely for the best possible outcome. To achieve successful collaboration, it is important to find individuals or groups who complement our strengths and weaknesses. By working with diverse perspectives and skill sets, we can tackle challenges from different angles and come up with innovative solutions. Additionally, fostering a collaborative environment promotes learning and personal growth, as we can learn from others' expertise and experiences.

In extreme rivalry, the focus shifts from achieving common goals to outdoing and undermining one another. This not only hampers progress but also creates a toxic environment that hinders creativity and teamwork. It is crucial to promote a healthy balance between competition and cooperation to ensure harmonious and productive collaboration. However, striking the right balance between competition and cooperation can also lead to positive outcomes, promoting a dynamic and thriving environment. The competition encourages organizations to strive for excellence, pushing them to innovate and improve their performance. On the other hand, cooperation fosters collaboration and teamwork. Let's explore what healthy competition provides and what cooperation provides because these are the main elements of competition.

Healthy competition provides:

1) Motivation and Improvement:

Healthy competition motivates individuals and teams to improve their skills and interpretation. The desire to beat others can drive innovation and the pursuit of excellence. For example, in the world of sports, athletes competing against each other push themselves to train harder, develop new techniques, and set higher goals to outperform their opponents. This competitive drive ultimately leads to the advancement of the sport and the achievement of new records.

2) Innovation and Creativity:

Competition often sparks innovation as individuals find better solutions, products, or services to gain a competitive edge. For instance, in the technology industry, companies constantly strive to outdo each other by developing innovative products that satisfy the ever-evolving needs of consumers. This competition has led to ground-breaking inventions like smartphones, virtual reality devices, and AI assistants, revolutionizing the way we communicate, work, and live our lives. This has ultimately resulted in significant advancements in technology and has greatly improved the quality of life for many individuals.

3) Efficiency and Productivity:

When individuals come together, there are more resources, customers, or market share that can drive efficiency and productivity. It encourages a focus on optimizing processes and utilizing resources effectively. It encourages a focus on optimizing processes and utilizing resources effectively, ultimately leading to greater output and success.

4) Personal Development:

In personal and professional contexts, healthy competition can contribute to individual development by pushing people out of their comfort zones and encouraging continuous learning. For example, in a workplace setting, a team of employees competing against each other to achieve sales targets can lead to increased productivity as they strive to outperform one another.

This healthy competition encourages individuals to continuously improve their skills and knowledge to stay ahead. Additionally, in an academic environment, students competing for top grades can drive personal growth by pushing themselves to study harder and explore new areas of knowledge. It can also foster a sense of achievement and personal satisfaction.

(Summary for the above concept)

Healthy competition drives motivation, innovation, efficiency, and personal development. It motivates individuals to improve skills, sparks creativity, and optimizes resources. It also encourages efficiency and productivity by focusing on optimizing processes and utilizing resources effectively. In both personal and professional contexts, it promotes continuous learning and growth.

What does collaboration provide?

1) Shared Goals and Resources:

Cooperation involves working together towards shared goals. It enables the pooling of resources, knowledge, and expertise for mutual benefit. For example, in composing a song, collaboration allows team members to come together and share their skills and resources to achieve a common goal. In this way, the final product is often more innovative and impactful than if each individual had worked alone. This could involve brainstorming sessions where everyone contributes their ideas and expertise or dividing tasks based on individual strengths to ensure efficient completion of the song. By collaborating and working towards a shared goal, individuals can leverage their collective resources and skills to produce high-quality work.

2) Teamwork:

Collaboration often leads to synergy, where the combined efforts of a group result in outcomes that are greater than the sum of individual contributions.

3) Conflict Resolution:

Cooperation is crucial for resolving conflicts and finding common ground. It promotes communication, understanding, and compromise in various situations. For example, in a software development project, a team of programmers with different expertise and strengths can come together to create a complex and innovative software solution. By pooling their knowledge and skills, they can design, code, test, and debug the software more efficiently and effectively than if each individual worked alone. This collaboration allows them to identify and address potential issues early on, resulting in a higher-quality final product.

4) Community Building:

Collaboration is the foundation of strong team of communities. When a programmers collaborates, they not only work towards a common goal but also build trust and friendship among themselves.

Thinking Higher than Trophies

This sense of community generates a positive work environment where members can freely interact, share ideas, and nurture each other's growth. Whether at the local or global level, working together on common issues can lead to positive social change and development.

(Summary for the above concept)

Cooperation involves working together towards shared goals, pooling resources, and promoting teamwork. It leads to synergy, conflict resolution, and community building. It promotes communication, understanding, and compromise, fostering positive social change and development at both local and global levels. What happens when healthy competition and cooperation come together? It creates trust within individuals. And results in a positive relationship, which helps individuals face risks and have a common solution to a problem. This also helps individuals pursue and climb the ladder of success. Have you ever played the game Treasure Hunt? In this game, the team has to give answers to the riddles asked in the chit.

And, if the answer to the riddle is correct, they will reach another checkpoint (here: chit), and step by step, they will be able to find the treasure. In the same way, in collaborative competition, the team has a common goal that can be reached step by step by achieving checkpoints. This team of individuals is like a mesh, which has to be handled with care and comfort. Things we should implement in collaborative competition: As we have seen, this concept is like a mesh, so we should implement some things to enhance the durability of this mesh. In collaborative competition, effective communication and cooperation among team members are crucial to successfully navigating through the checkpoints. Each individual's strengths and weaknesses must be taken into consideration to ensure a harmonious and efficient workflow.

Additionally, fostering a supportive and inclusive environment within the team can enhance morale and encourage creative problem-solving. Furthermore, establishing clear roles and responsibilities for each team member can help streamline the workflow and minimize confusion. Regular team meetings and open lines of communication are also essential to address any challenges or conflicts that may arise, allowing for timely resolution and a stronger overall team dynamic.

Moreover, establishing clear goals and expectations can help align team members toward a common objective, stimulating a sense of purpose and direction. Regular team meetings and feedback sessions can also boost open communication and allow for the identification and resolution of any issues or conflicts that may arise.

(Summary of the 3rd Chapter)

Collaborative competition is a blend of collaboration and competition to achieve common goals or mutual benefits. This concept encourages creativity, productivity, and success by harnessing the positive aspects of competition. Healthy competition drives motivation, innovation, efficiency, and personal development by promoting creativity and optimizing resources. Cooperation provides shared goals and resources, teamwork, conflict resolution, and community building. Cooperation also fosters a sense of unity and trust among individuals and groups. When healthy competition and cooperation come together, it creates trust and positive relationships, helping individuals face risks and find common solutions. Incorporating effective communication and cooperation among team members is crucial to successfully navigating through checkpoints and achieving common goals.

Fostering a supportive and inclusive environment within the team can enhance morale and encourage creative problem-solving. By striking the right balance between competition and cooperation, organizations can foster a dynamic and thriving environment that promotes continuous improvement and adaptability to ever-changing trends. By fostering a supportive and collaborative environment, individuals can learn from one another, develop new skills, and gain a deeper understanding of various industries.

Conclusion:

In conclusion, collaborative competition offers a transformative approach to competition that emphasizes cooperation, teamwork, and mutual benefit. By harnessing the power of both competition and collaboration, individuals and organizations can unlock new opportunities, drive innovation, and achieve collective success. As we navigate the complexities of today's world, embracing collaboration as a cornerstone of competition is key to build a brighter and more prosperous future.

Would you happen to know? Some people in a team still have the mindset to benefit themselves.

Thinking Higher than Trophies

To break free from the trophy mindset, team members must shift their focus from individual achievements to collective success. In the coming chapter, we will see some strategies to overcome the trophy mindset.

Chapter 4

Escaping the Trophy Trap

"Thinking Higher than the Trophies"

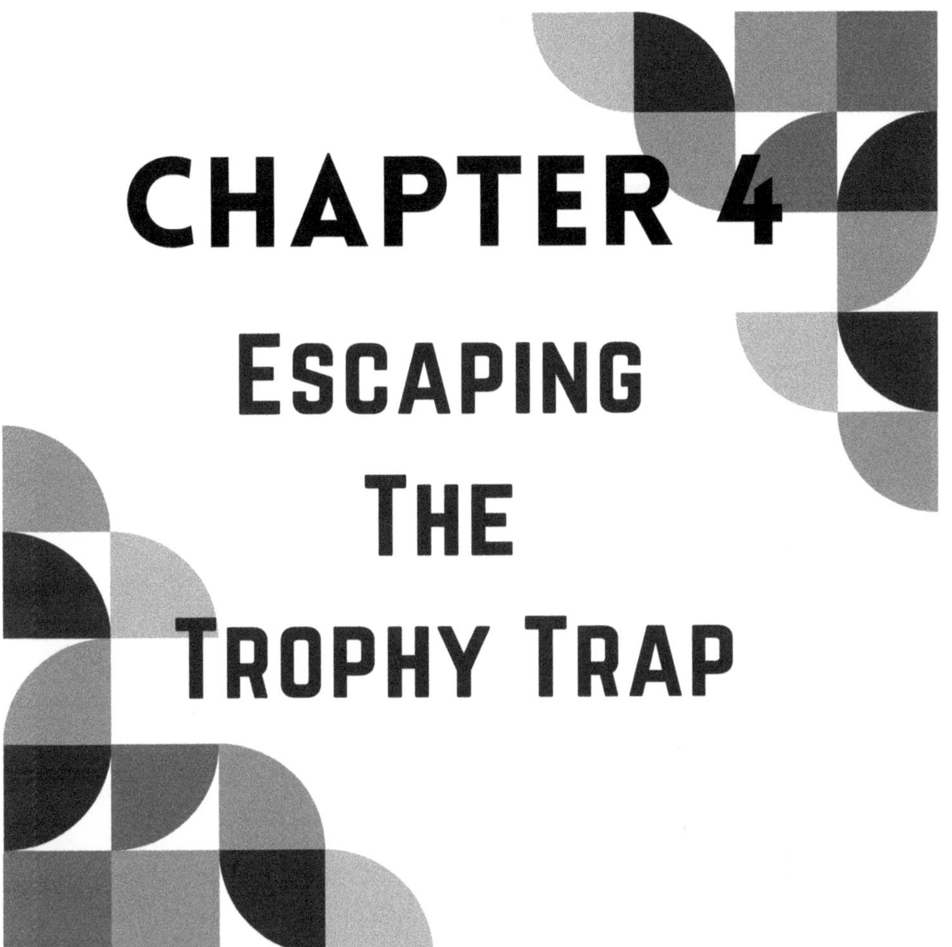

CHAPTER 4
ESCAPING THE TROPHY TRAP

In previous chapters, we have seen:

Chapter 1:

- What is competition?
- Steps of competition (how our brain gets occupied)
- The good and bad sides of a competition Origin of competitive spirit
- How competition affects our psychology

Chapter 2:

A New View of Competition Adaptation Technique.

Chapter 3:

- Introduction to a New Concept
- What does healthy competition provide?
- What does collaboration provide?
- What happens when healthy competition and collaboration come together?
- Things we should implement in a collaborative competition for a more effective and successful outcome.

The list of points above provides a quick rundown of what we discovered. But do you know? Within a team, there are still individuals who only think about themselves. We've now entered a new chapter.

This chapter will teach us the following:

- Why should we overcome the trophy mentality? How can I overcome a trophy mentality?

- And, a tonne of other fascinating things that will help us grow and succeed together as individuals.

Why should we break free from a "trophy mindset"? Or how can we strike a balance between personal success and shared success?

Breaking free from a "trophy mind-set" is crucial because it promotes a narrow focus on individual achievements and undermines the importance of collaboration and collective growth. By shifting our perspective towards shared success, we can foster a more inclusive and supportive environment where personal accomplishments are celebrated alongside the accomplishments of others.

Do you know? A "trophy mind-set" can also cause us to miss out on important opportunities to learn and develop new abilities that will improve the skills that have earned so much recognition. It's critical to keep in mind that success is determined not by the number of awards we receive but instead by the path we choose and the abilities we develop along the way. Only by constantly challenging ourselves and striving for improvement can we truly reach our full potential.

The concept of a "trophy mind-set" and its impact on personal growth:

A trophy mind-set that solely focuses on external recognition can hinder one's willingness to take risks, learn from failures, and embrace new challenges. When we are solely focused on external recognition, we may become hesitant to take risks because failure could tarnish our trophy collection. This fear of failure can prevent us from stepping outside of our comfort zones and embracing new challenges that have the potential to expand our abilities and lead to personal growth. By prioritizing awards over personal development, we limit ourselves from experiencing the valuable lessons that come from learning through trial and error. We miss out on the opportunity to reach our full potential.

And, do you know, when we start collaborating with other individuals, our mistakes don't come directly in front of other people, and because of this, we can come out of our comfort zone anytime.

A highlight on the values of embracing failure:

Accepting failure helps us grow stronger and learn from our errors, which eventually results in more success down the road. By encouraging us to take chances and go beyond our comfort zones, it helps us develop self-assurance and confidence in our skills. Furthermore, by owning up to our mistakes and drawing lessons from them, we may encourage others to follow suit and foster an innovative and growing culture.

According to research, four studies were done to understand how a parent's pressure can increase their failure and also demotivate their child.

Let's see what these studies highlight...

Study 1:

In Study 1, researchers found that parents can view failure as debilitating or enhancing and that these failure mind-sets predict parenting practices and, in turn, children's intelligence mind-sets. The results showed that parents who viewed failure as debilitating were more likely to have controlling behaviours toward their children, which ultimately increased their failure and also demotivation. On the other hand, parents who viewed failure as an opportunity for growth were more likely to have supportive and empowering behaviours toward their children, leading to increased resilience and motivation.

Study 2:

Study 2 probed more deeply into how parents display failure mind-sets.

Study 3:

Study 3 has Two Parts:

- Study 3a
- Study 3b

Study 3a:

We found that children can indeed accurately perceive their failure mind-sets but not their parents' intelligence mind-sets.

Study 3b:

Study 3b showed that children's perceptions of their parents' failure mind-sets also predicted their intelligence mind-sets.

Study 4:

Finally, Study 4 showed a causal effect of parents' failure mind-sets on their responses to their children's hypothetical failure. Overall, parents who see failure as debilitating focus on their children's performance and ability rather than on their children's learning, and their children, in turn, tend to believe that intelligence is fixed rather than malleable. As a result, they may avoid challenges and give up easily when faced with obstacles.

But you might be wondering, Why is this point here?

So, according to the points given above, we can conclude that the trophy mind-set and failure are linked. Because people who believe in the trophy mind-set don't like failures. But failure is one of our building blocks for success. But, because of this mind-set, people may avoid taking risks and miss out on valuable learning opportunities. The trophy mind-set limits people and makes them stay away from failure to maintain their self-image and avoid the discomfort of not being perfect. This fixed mind-set can hinder personal growth and development, as individuals are less likely to challenge themselves and strive for improvement. Additionally, it can lead to a fear of failure and reluctance to try new things, ultimately limiting one's potential for success. The best thing is that using collaboration instead of a trophy mind-set helps us to hide our mistakes, and our mistakes don't come directly in front of other people. Because of this, we can come out of our comfort zone at any time. This allows us to grow and learn from our experiences without fear of judgment or failure. By embracing collaboration instead of a trophy mind-set, individuals can foster a sense of support and encouragement from those around them. This creates an environment where mistakes are seen as opportunities for growth and learning, rather than sources of shame or embarrassment. Ultimately, this mind-set shift can unlock one's true potential and enable personal growth and development in ways that a trophy mind- set cannot. Embracing a growth mind-set allows us to value the journey and the lessons learned, rather than just the result.

But how do you overcome a trophy mind-set?

The easiest way to get past a trophy mind-set is to spend some time for self-introspection.

Thinking Higher than Trophies

What does this mean?

Let's explore the meaning of taking time for self-reflection

What is Self-Reflection?

It is having the realization that what is the pursuit of gaining achievements? Is it to fill your closet, or is it for some other reason? Assess oneself, and be sure that your intentions and conscience are correct. If your conscience and intentions are right, then winning will boost your motivation more and more. And you will also not be affected after losing. Having the right intentions is crucial for personal fulfilment and inner satisfaction. When your intentions align with your values and principles, even if you don't win, you can still find contentment in knowing that you stayed true to yourself. It is this self- satisfaction that ultimately leads to a sense of fulfilment and long-term happiness. However, if your intentions are incorrect, you will attain fleeting happiness rather than self-satisfaction. You can learn from your failures and turn them into stepping stones for future success if you keep an optimistic outlook, no matter what happens. Recall that real development results from accepting successes and setbacks with equal tenacity. Did you know that people who receive trophies for a variety of reasons could become anxious if their goals aren't met? To be content with yourself, you must evaluate yourself. Because we are gaining more and more achievements, we forget to take time to master new skills or enhance existing ones. And, in due time, the people you are working are taking advantage of your mindset by getting more apt and productive.

The second method of breaking free of the trophy mindset is linked with the first method. The second method is to "cope yourself up after losing." Research has proven that "winning" doesn't affect your mind-set, but one loss can shake your confidence and impact your mindset. That is the reason why I chose this method of coping with yourself after losing. If you make yourself strong to handle loss, you will not be impacted easily by it.

But how do I make myself mentally strong enough to handle loss?

Let's see some steps that will make you a mentally strong person who can handle a loss in a competition:

1. Accepting your loss
2. Keep yourself happy.
3. Equip yourself for the next competition.

Accepting your loss, keeping yourself happy, and equipping yourself for the next competition are ways to deal with losing that will allow you to feel optimistic about your participation and ready to face the next challenge.

Accepting your loss:

Accepting your loss is a crucial aspect of personal growth and resilience. It involves acknowledging and accepting the reality of a setback or disappointment, allowing yourself to experience the associated emotions, and ultimately finding a way to move forward. This process often fosters strength, learning, and a renewed sense of purpose.

Keeping yourself happy:

Maintaining happiness after a loss involves nurturing self-care, focusing on positive aspects, and embracing resilience. Engage in activities that bring joy, surround yourself with supportive people, and allow yourself time to heal. Cultivate a positive mind-set by acknowledging achievements, setting realistic goals, and finding meaning in the experience. Practising gratitude and mindfulness can also contribute to sustaining happiness in challenging times. Remember to be patient with yourself throughout this process.

Equipping yourself after a loss:

Equipping yourself after a loss involves building resilience, learning from the experience, and developing coping mechanisms. Assess the lessons gained from the loss, identify areas for personal growth, and set realistic goals. Cultivate a support system, seek professional guidance, and prioritize self-care. Embrace adaptability and a positive mind- set, as these traits can empower you to navigate future challenges with greater strength and insight. Remember to be kind to yourself and celebrate your progress along the way.

(Summary of the 4th Chapter)

In this chapter, we explored the concept of competition and its impact on our psychology. We discuss the importance of overcoming the "trophy mentality" and how it can hinder personal growth and development. A "trophy mind-set" is a narrow focus on individual achievements that undermines the importance of collaboration and collective growth. By shifting our perspective towards shared success, we can foster a more inclusive and supportive environment where personal accomplishments are celebrated alongside the accomplishments of others. A trophy mind-set can hinder one's willingness to take risks, learn from failures, and embrace new challenges. When we are solely focused on external recognition, we may become hesitant to take risks because failure could tarnish our trophy collection. By prioritizing awards over personal development, we limit ourselves from experiencing the valuable lessons that come from learning through trial and error. By embracing collaboration instead of a trophy mind-set, individuals can foster a sense of support and encouragement from those around them. This creates an environment where mistakes are seen as opportunities for growth and learning, rather than sources of shame or embarrassment. Ultimately, this mind-set shift can unlock one's true potential and enable personal growth and development in ways that a trophy mind-set cannot.

Embracing a growth mind-set allows us to value the journey and the lessons learned, rather than just the result. The easiest way to get past a trophy mind-set is to spend some time for self-introspection. The meaning of taking time for self-reflection is having the realization that what is the pursuit of gaining achievements? It is about personal growth and development. Is it to fill your closet, or is it for some other reason? Assess oneself, and be sure that your intentions and conscience are correct. If your conscience and intentions are right, winning will boost your motivation more, and you'll not be affected after losing. Having the right intentions is crucial for personal fulfilment and inner satisfaction. When your intentions align with your values and principles, even if you don't win, you can still find contentment in knowing that you stayed true to yourself. This self-satisfaction ultimately leads to a sense of fulfilment and long-term happiness. However, if your intentions are incorrect, you will attain fleeting happiness rather than self-satisfaction. You can learn from your failures and turn them into stepping stones for future success if you keep an optimistic outlook, no matter what happens. Remember that real development results from accepting successes and setbacks with equal tenacity.

The second method of breaking free of the trophy mind-set is to "cope yourself up after losing." Research has shown that "winning" doesn't affect your mind-set, but one loss can shake your confidence and impact your mind-set. To make yourself mentally strong enough to handle loss, follow these steps:

1. Accept your loss.

2. Keep yourself happy.

3. Equip yourself for the next competition.

Maintaining happiness after a loss involves nurturing self-care, focusing on positive aspects, and embracing resilience. Engage in activities that bring joy, surround yourself with supportive people, and allow yourself time to heal. Cultivate a positive mindset by acknowledging achievements, setting realistic goals, and finding meaning in the experience. Practising gratitude and mindfulness can also contribute to sustaining happiness in challenging times. Equipping yourself after a loss involves building resilience, learning from the experience, and developing coping mechanisms. Assess the lessons gained from the loss, identify areas for personal growth, and set realistic goals. Cultivate a support system, seek professional guidance, and prioritize self-care. Embrace adaptability and a positive mind-set, as these traits can empower you to navigate future challenges with greater strength and insight.

Conclusion and Call to Action:

In conclusion, overcoming the trophy mentality is essential for personal growth and collective success. By embracing failure, fostering collaboration, and adopting a growth mind-set, individuals can unlock their full potential and thrive in a dynamic and ever- changing world.

Conclusion

Words of Comfort

"Thinking Higher than the Trophies"

CONCLUSION

(Words of Comfort)

Throughout the pages of this book, we've embarked on an enlightening journey through the realms of competition, collaboration, and personal growth. From dissecting the origins of competitive spirit to delving into the intricacies of productive competition and the pitfalls of a trophy mind-set, we've uncovered a wealth of insights and practical strategies for navigating the complex landscape of success.

As we conclude our journey, let us carry forward the lessons learned and embrace a future characterized by collaboration, compassion, and continuous growth. Let us cultivate resilience in the face of adversity, harness the power of mentorship and networking, and prioritize emotional intelligence and mindfulness in our pursuit of excellence.

Above all, always remember that success is not a destination but a journey—a journey shaped by the relationships we forge, the challenges we overcome, and the lessons we learn along the way. So, let us embark on this journey together, supporting one another, lifting each other, and celebrating the collective achievements that propel us toward a brighter tomorrow.

I would like to end this book with a quote and a poem.

Quote:

"Success is not about standing alone at the apex of achievement but about lifting others along the journey."

-Sinai Jagdale

Poem:

In life's big game, we play and try.
Sometimes we win, sometimes we cry.
We learn to share and work as one.
In teamwork's dance, we find the fun.

From wanting trophies, we can see:
It's more about you and me.
We learn from falls, we learn from strife,
And pick ourselves back up in life.

To think just of ourselves is tough.
But together, we have enough.
We learn from trying, even when we fail.
And we will find success when we set sail.

With each new dawn, a chance to grow,
To face the challenges we don't yet know.

Thinking Higher than Trophies

In every stumble, a lesson lies,

Guiding us forward, under open skies.

Through laughter's echo and tears'

embrace, We navigate life's complex

maze.

With every setback, a door unbarred,

Leading us closer to dreams unscarred.

So let's be kind; let's lend a hand.

And help each other understand.

In working together, we find our way.

And make our world a brighter day.

-Sinai Jagdale

Thinking Higher than Trophies

Thank you for joining me on this exploration of competition, collaboration, and personal growth. May the insights gained inspire you to embrace your full potential and make a positive impact on the world around you. Remember, we are all on this journey called life together. By supporting and uplifting one another, we can achieve great things and overcome any obstacles that come our way. Let's continue to spread kindness, empathy, and understanding wherever we go, and watch as our collective efforts create a more harmonious and compassionate world for all. Thank you for being a part of this beautiful journey towards personal growth and global unity.

So this is SINAI JAGDALE signing off, I hope you'll like this book. So, see you soon in the next book...

www.ingramcontent.com/pod-product-compliance
Lightning Source LLC
LaVergne TN
LVHW021144160826
845679LV00023B/2040